Whipped Delights

A Guide to Irresistible Cream Pancakes

WHIPPED DELIGHTS

First edition. December 15, 2023.

ISBN: 979-8215297827

Written by Jose Maria.

Table of Contents

Jose Maria

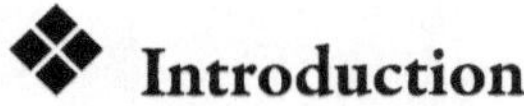 **Introduction**

A. Brief History of Pancakes

Pancakes, a beloved breakfast staple, have a rich history that spans cultures and centuries. Traced back to ancient civilizations, various forms of pancakes have been enjoyed worldwide. The earliest known references date back to ancient Greece, where a form of pancake called "tagenites" was made with wheat flour, olive oil, honey, and curdled milk.

Throughout history, pancakes have evolved and taken on different names and variations, from French crepes to Russian blinis. They've been a symbol of celebration, often associated with religious festivals and feasts.

B. The Versatility of Pancakes

One of the reasons pancakes have endured through time is their incredible versatility. From sweet to savory, thick to thin, pancakes can be adapted to suit a myriad of tastes and occasions. They've found their way onto breakfast tables, brunch spreads, and even dessert menus.

The simplicity of the pancake batter allows for creative additions, making it a canvas for culinary experimentation. Whether you prefer a classic stack with maple syrup or a more adventurous flavor combination, pancakes are a delightful blank slate.

C. Why Cream Pancakes Stand Out

While traditional pancakes are undeniably delicious, the addition of whipped cream introduces a luscious and indulgent element. Cream pancakes elevate the classic breakfast dish to a new level of decadence. The creamy texture not only enhances the pancake itself but also serves as a perfect complement to a variety of toppings and fillings.

Cream pancakes are a celebration of texture and flavor, offering a velvety richness that pairs wonderfully with both sweet and savory ingredients. The incorporation of whipping cream into the batter results in a fluffy and tender pancake that is sure to captivate your taste buds.

In the following sections, we'll delve into the art of crafting these irresistible cream pancakes, exploring different variations, flavor combinations, and even healthier alternatives to suit every palate and occasion. Let's embark on a journey of pancake perfection!

Chapter(1) Getting Started

A. Essential Ingredients
   All-Purpose Flour

- 2 cups of all-purpose flour form the base of the pancake batter.

Baking Powder

- 1 tablespoon of baking powder adds leavening, ensuring the pancakes rise to perfection.

Sugar

- 2 tablespoons of sugar provide a touch of sweetness to balance the flavors.

Salt

- 1/2 teaspoon of salt enhances the overall taste of the pancakes.

Eggs

- 2 large eggs act as a binding agent, contributing to the structure of the pancakes.

Milk

- 1 1/2 cups of milk create a smooth and pourable batter. Feel free to use your preferred type of milk.

Vanilla Extract

- 1 teaspoon of vanilla extract imparts a fragrant and sweet aroma to the pancakes.

Whipping Cream

- 1/2 cup of whipping cream elevates the texture, making the pancakes delightfully creamy.

B. Equipment Needed
Mixing Bowls

- Large mixing bowls for combining dry and wet ingredients separately, ensuring a well-mixed batter.

Whisk

- A whisk for smoothly blending the batter, preventing lumps and ensuring a consistent texture.

Griddle or Skillet

- A flat, non-stick griddle or skillet for cooking the pancakes evenly. Adjust the temperature to medium for best results.

Spatula

- A spatula for easy flipping of the pancakes. Ensure it's heat-resistant and wide enough to support the entire pancake.

Now that you have gathered your ingredients and equipment, let's dive into the step-by-step instructions to create the perfect basic cream pancake.

Chapter(2) Basic Cream Pancake Recipe

A. Step-by-Step Instructions

Prepare the Dry Ingredients:

In a large mixing bowl, whisk together 2 cups of all-purpose flour, 1 tablespoon of baking powder, 2 tablespoons of sugar, and 1/2 teaspoon of salt.

Combine Wet Ingredients:

In another bowl, beat 2 eggs and then add 1 1/2 cups of milk, 1 teaspoon of vanilla extract, and 1/2 cup of whipping cream. Mix until well combined.

Create the Batter:

Pour the wet ingredients into the dry ingredients and gently stir until just combined. Be careful not to overmix; a few lumps are okay. Let the batter rest for 5 minutes.

Preheat the Griddle or Skillet:

Heat a non-stick griddle or skillet over medium heat. Lightly grease it with butter or cooking spray.

Cook the Pancakes:

Pour 1/4 cup of batter onto the griddle for each pancake. Cook until bubbles form on the surface, then flip and cook the other side until golden brown.

Serve Warm:

Once cooked, transfer the pancakes to a plate. Serve warm with your favorite toppings.

B. Tips for Achieving the Perfect Fluffy Texture

Don't Overmix:

Gently fold the wet and dry ingredients together. Overmixing can result in tough pancakes.

Let the Batter Rest:

Allowing the batter to rest for a few minutes before cooking helps activate the leavening agents and ensures fluffier pancakes.

Use Fresh Baking Powder:

Ensure your baking powder is fresh for optimal rising. If it's been sitting in the pantry for a while, consider replacing it.

Adjust Heat Carefully:

Maintain a medium heat on the griddle or skillet. Too high heat can lead to uneven cooking.

C. Variations for Different Dietary Preferences

Gluten-Free Option:

Substitute the all-purpose flour with a gluten-free flour blend. Check the consistency of the batter and adjust as needed.

Dairy-Free Option:

Use a dairy-free milk alternative (almond, soy, coconut) and a non-dairy whipped cream substitute.

Egg-Free Option:

Replace the eggs with a suitable egg replacer or mashed bananas/applesauce for binding.

Low-Sugar Option:

Reduce the amount of sugar in the recipe or use a sugar substitute for a healthier alternative.

Feel free to experiment with these variations to cater to different dietary needs and preferences. Now, you have the foundation for delightful cream pancakes – let your creativity shine!

Chapter(3) Flavorful Additions

A. Fresh Fruit Toppings

Berry Bliss:

Top your cream pancakes with a medley of fresh berries such as strawberries, blueberries, and raspberries. Drizzle with a touch of honey or maple syrup.

Tropical Paradise:

Sliced bananas, mango chunks, and a sprinkle of shredded coconut create a tropical delight. Finish with a dollop of whipped cream.

Citrus Sensation:

Orange segments and a light dusting of powdered sugar add a zesty twist. Garnish with mint leaves for a burst of freshness.

B. Nuts and Seeds for Crunch

Nutty Delight:

Toasted almonds or pecans sprinkled over the pancakes provide a delightful crunch. Add a drizzle of caramel for extra indulgence.

Seeds Galore:

Sunflower seeds or pumpkin seeds add a nutty flavor and textural contrast. Pair with a honey or yogurt drizzle for balance.

C. Chocolate Swirls and Chips

Classic Chocolate Chip:

Fold chocolate chips into the pancake batter for a classic treat. Serve with a generous swirl of chocolate sauce and a scoop of vanilla ice cream.

Decadent Nutella Swirl:

Swirl Nutella into the pancake batter before cooking. Top with hazelnuts and a dusting of cocoa powder for a luxurious experience.

D. Savory Twists for a Unique Experience
   Bacon and Maple Syrup:
Crispy bacon crumbles on top of cream pancakes, drizzled with maple syrup, strike the perfect balance between sweet and savory.
   Herbed Cream Cheese:
Mix chopped herbs (such as chives or parsley) into cream cheese and spread between pancake layers. Serve with smoked salmon for a sophisticated twist.
   Savory Veggie Medley:
Sautéed mushrooms, spinach, and cherry tomatoes create a savory pancake delight. Top with a dollop of sour cream or Greek yogurt.

Feel free to mix and match these additions to create your own signature cream pancake creations. Whether you have a sweet tooth or prefer a savory experience, these flavorful toppings and twists will take your cream pancakes to the next level!

Chapter(4) Gourmet Cream Pancake Creations

A. Stuffed Pancakes with Cream Filling

Cream-Filled Berry Burst:

Prepare a cream filling by whipping together cream cheese, powdered sugar, and a splash of vanilla extract. Spoon the filling onto a pancake, top with fresh berries, and sandwich with another pancake. Dust with powdered sugar.

Nutty Chocolate Surprise:

Spread a layer of chocolate hazelnut spread on a pancake, sprinkle chopped hazelnuts, and top with another pancake. Finish with a drizzle of warm chocolate ganache.

B. Layered Pancake Cakes

Strawberry Shortcake Stack:

Alternate layers of cream pancakes with slices of fresh strawberries and a dollop of whipped cream. Finish with a dusting of powdered sugar.

Caramel Apple Stack:

Cook diced apples with cinnamon until tender. Layer cream pancakes with the caramelized apples and a caramel drizzle. Top with a scoop of vanilla ice cream.

C. Pancake Sandwiches with Delectable Spreads

Peanut Butter Banana Bliss:

Spread peanut butter on one pancake, add banana slices, and sandwich with another pancake. Drizzle with honey and sprinkle with chopped peanuts.

Raspberry Almond Elegance:

Spread almond butter on a pancake, layer with fresh raspberries, and sandwich with another pancake. Finish with a sprinkle of sliced almonds.

D. Served with Complementary Sauces

Vanilla Bourbon Maple Syrup:

Mix pure maple syrup with a splash of vanilla extract and a tablespoon of bourbon. Warm the mixture and drizzle over your cream pancakes for a decadent touch.

Berry Coulis Drizzle:

Blend mixed berries with a bit of sugar and strain to create a smooth coulis. Drizzle this vibrant berry sauce over your cream pancakes for a burst of flavor.

Citrus Infused Honey:

Warm honey with a hint of citrus zest (lemon or orange). Drizzle over the pancakes for a refreshing and fragrant addition.

These gourmet cream pancake creations are perfect for special occasions or when you want to treat yourself to a luxurious breakfast experience. The combinations are endless, so feel free to experiment and find your favorite indulgent stack!

Chapter(5) Special Occasion Cream Pancakes

A. Holiday-Inspired Recipes

Christmas Cranberry Cream Pancakes

Ingredients:

- Cream pancake batter
- Fresh cranberries
- Orange zest
- Ground cinnamon
- Whipped cream

Instructions:

1. Fold fresh cranberries into the pancake batter for a burst of color and tartness.
2. Add a pinch of ground cinnamon to the batter.
3. Cook the pancakes until golden brown.
4. Top with a sprinkle of orange zest and a dollop of whipped cream.
5. Valentine's Day Strawberry Cream Pancakes

Ingredients:

- Cream pancake batter
- Fresh strawberries, sliced
- Dark chocolate chips
- Strawberry syrup
- Whipped cream

Instructions:

1. Mix dark chocolate chips into the pancake batter for a hint of indulgence.
2. Cook the pancakes until the chocolate chips melt and create swirls.
3. Layer with fresh strawberry slices.
4. Drizzle with strawberry syrup and top with whipped cream.

B. Birthday Surprises
Funfetti Cream Pancakes
Ingredients:

- Cream pancake batter
- Colorful sprinkles (nonpareils)
- Vanilla frosting
- Additional sprinkles for decoration

Instructions:

1. Gently fold colorful sprinkles into the pancake batter.
2. Cook the pancakes until the sprinkles create a funfetti effect.
3. Stack the pancakes and spread a layer of vanilla frosting between each layer.
4. Top with additional sprinkles for a festive touch.
5. Birthday Cake Batter Pancakes

Ingredients:

- Cream pancake batter
- Yellow cake mix
- Sprinkles
- Vanilla glaze (powdered sugar, milk, and vanilla extract)

Instructions:

1. Mix a small amount of yellow cake mix into the pancake batter for a cake batter flavor.
2. Add colorful sprinkles to the batter.
3. Cook the pancakes until fluffy and golden brown.
4. Drizzle with a vanilla glaze made from powdered sugar, milk, and vanilla extract.

These special occasion cream pancake recipes add a festive and celebratory touch to your breakfast or brunch, making them perfect for holidays and birthdays. Enjoy these delightful treats with your loved ones!

Chapter(6) International Flavors

A. Tiramisu-Inspired Cream Pancakes
   Ingredients:

- Cream pancake batter
- Instant espresso powder
- Cocoa powder
- Mascarpone cheese
- Coffee liqueur (optional)
- Whipped cream

Instructions:

1. Prepare the cream pancake batter.
2. Dissolve 1 tablespoon of instant espresso powder in a small amount of hot water. Add this liqueur (optional).
3. Sandwich the pancakes with layers of the mascarpone mixture.
4. Dust with cocoa powder and top with a generous dollop of whipped cream.
5. to the pancake batter.
6. Cook the pancakes until golden brown.
7. In a separate bowl, mix mascarpone cheese with a splash of coffee

B. Matcha Green Tea Cream Pancakes
Ingredients:

- Cream pancake batter
- Matcha green tea powder
- Sweetened red bean paste
- Matcha glaze (powdered sugar, milk, and matcha powder)
- Toasted sesame seeds (optional)

Instructions:

1. Prepare the cream pancake batter.
2. Whisk in 1-2 tablespoons of matcha green tea powder into the batter.
3. Cook the pancakes until light and fluffy.
4. Spread a layer of sweetened red bean paste between the pancakes.
5. Drizzle with a matcha glaze made from powdered sugar, milk, and matcha powder.
6. Optionally, sprinkle toasted sesame seeds on top for added crunch.

C. Coconut and Tropical Fruit Fusion
Ingredients:

- Cream pancake batter
- Coconut milk
- Pineapple chunks
- Mango slices
- Shredded coconut
- Passion fruit syrup

Instructions:

1. Prepare the cream pancake batter, substituting some of the milk with coconut milk for a tropical twist.
2. Cook the pancakes until golden and fragrant.
3. Layer the pancakes with chunks of pineapple and slices of mango.
4. Sprinkle shredded coconut on top for added texture.
5. Drizzle with passion fruit syrup for a burst of exotic flavor.

These international-inspired cream pancake recipes bring unique and delightful flavors from around the world to your breakfast table. Enjoy a taste of Italy, Japan, and the tropics with these delicious creations!

Chapter(7) Healthier Alternatives

A. Whole Wheat Cream Pancakes
   Ingredients:

- Whole wheat flour
- Baking powder
- Honey or maple syrup (as a natural sweetener)
- Salt
- Eggs
- Milk
- Vanilla extract
- Whipping cream

Instructions:

1. Replace all-purpose flour with whole wheat flour in the cream pancake batter.
2. Use honey or maple syrup as a natural sweetener instead of granulated sugar.
3. Follow the standard cream pancake recipe for the remaining ingredients.
4. Cook the pancakes until they achieve a golden-brown color.
5. Top with your favorite fresh fruit or a dollop of Greek yogurt for added nutrition.

B. Oatmeal and Yogurt Cream Pancakes
   Ingredients:

- Rolled oats (blended into a coarse flour)
- Baking powder

- Greek yogurt
- Eggs
- Milk
- Vanilla extract
- Whipping cream

Instructions:

1. Blend rolled oats into a coarse flour to replace part or all of the all-purpose flour in the cream pancake batter.
2. Add Greek yogurt to the batter for a protein boost and a creamy texture.
3. Follow the standard cream pancake recipe for the remaining ingredients.
4. Cook the pancakes until they are cooked through and have a nice texture.
5. Serve with a drizzle of honey and a handful of mixed berries for a nutritious twist.

C. Low-Sugar Options for Guilt-Free Indulgence
Ingredients:

- Almond flour or coconut flour
- Baking powder
- Monk fruit sweetener or Stevia (as a low-calorie sweetener)
- Salt
- Eggs
- Almond milk or coconut milk
- Vanilla extract
- Whipping cream

Instructions:

1. Substitute almond flour or coconut flour for the all-purpose

flour in the cream pancake batter.

2. Use a low-calorie sweetener like monk fruit or Stevia instead of regular sugar.
3. Follow the standard cream pancake recipe for the remaining ingredients.
4. Cook the pancakes until they are golden brown and cooked through.
5. Top with a dollop of whipped cream and a sprinkle of fresh berries for added sweetness.

These healthier alternatives to cream pancakes offer a guilt-free indulgence without compromising on flavor or texture. Enjoy these nutritious twists to start your day on a wholesome note!

Chapter(8) Troubleshooting Guide

A. Common Issues and Solutions

- **Issue:** Pancakes are too dense.

✓ **Solution:** Ensure you are not overmixing the batter; a few lumps are acceptable. Additionally, check that your baking powder is fresh and active.

- **Issue:** Pancakes are too thin and spread out.

✓ **Solution**: Make sure your griddle or skillet is at the correct temperature. Too high heat can cause the batter to spread too much. Adjust and try cooking at a slightly lower temperature.

- **Issue:** Pancakes are sticking to the griddle.

✓ **Solution:** Ensure your griddle is well-greased. Use a non-stick cooking spray or a small amount of butter before pouring the batter.

- **Issue:** Unevenly cooked pancakes.

✓ **Solution:** Maintain a consistent heat level on the griddle. Ensure all pancakes are of a similar size for even cooking. Flip them when bubbles form on the surface.

- **Issue:** Pancakes are too dry.

✓ **Solution:** Double-check the cooking time; overcooking can lead to dry pancakes. Adjust the heat and cook until just done. Consider incorporating more liquid into the batter if needed.

B. Tips for Perfecting Your Cream Pancakes

Use Fresh Ingredients:

Ensure that your baking powder, eggs, and other perishable items are fresh. This contributes to the overall quality of the pancakes.

Room Temperature Ingredients:

Allow ingredients like eggs and milk to come to room temperature before mixing. This promotes even blending and better incorporation into the batter.

Do Not Overmix:

Gently fold the wet and dry ingredients until just combined. Overmixing can result in tough pancakes.

Let the Batter Rest:

Allow the batter to rest for a few minutes before cooking. This helps activate the leavening agents and improves the texture.

Adjust Heat Accordingly:

Experiment with the griddle or skillet temperature. Too high heat can lead to uneven cooking, while too low heat may result in soggy pancakes.

Customize Toppings:

Have fun experimenting with different toppings and fillings. The versatility of cream pancakes allows for a wide range of creative additions.

Experiment with Flavors:

Try different extracts, spices, or flavored creams to enhance the taste of your pancakes. Creativity is key!

Practice Makes Perfect:

Perfecting pancakes may take a bit of practice. Adjustments to the recipe and technique can be made based on your preferences.

Remember, making the perfect cream pancakes is a delightful journey of trial and error. Don't be afraid to get creative and find your unique spin on this classic breakfast treat!

Chapter(9) Seasonal Sensations

A. Pumpkin Spice Cream Pancakes for Fall
Ingredients:

- Cream pancake batter
- Pumpkin puree
- Pumpkin spice (cinnamon, nutmeg, cloves)
- Brown sugar
- Whipping cream

Instructions:

1. Prepare the cream pancake batter.
2. Fold in a half cup of pumpkin puree, a teaspoon of pumpkin spice, and a tablespoon of brown sugar into the batter.
3. Cook the pancakes until golden brown.
4. Top with a dollop of whipped cream and an extra sprinkle of pumpkin spice.

B. Fresh Berry Delights for Summer Mornings
Ingredients:

- Cream pancake batter
- Mixed fresh berries (strawberries, blueberries, raspberries)
- Lemon zest
- Honey
- Whipping cream

Instructions:

1. Prepare the cream pancake batter.
2. Cook the pancakes until they are golden brown.
3. Top with a generous mix of fresh berries and a sprinkle of

lemon zest.
4. Drizzle with honey and finish with a dollop of whipped cream.

C. Apple Cinnamon Cream Pancakes for Cozy Winter Breakfasts
Ingredients:

- Cream pancake batter
- Apple, peeled and finely chopped
- Ground cinnamon
- Brown sugar
- Whipping cream

Instructions:

1. Prepare the cream pancake batter.
2. Mix in the chopped apple, a teaspoon of ground cinnamon, and a tablespoon of brown sugar into the batter.
3. Cook the pancakes until they have a warm, comforting aroma.
4. Top with a dollop of whipped cream and an extra sprinkle of cinnamon.

These seasonal sensations bring the flavors of fall, summer, and winter to your breakfast table. Embrace the changing seasons with these delicious and comforting cream pancake variations. Enjoy the taste of each season in every delightful bite!

Chapter(10) International Delights

A. French-Inspired Crème Fraîche Pancakes
   Ingredients:

- Cream pancake batter
- Crème fraîche
- Fresh berries (raspberries, blueberries)
- Honey
- Slivered almonds

Instructions:

1. Prepare the cream pancake batter.
2. Cook the pancakes until golden brown.
3. Spread a layer of crème fraîche between each pancake.
4. Top with fresh berries, drizzle with honey, and sprinkle with slivered almonds for a touch of elegance.

B. Japanese-Style Matcha Cream Dorayaki
   Ingredients:

- Cream pancake batter
- Matcha green tea powder
- Sweet red bean paste
- Whipping cream
- Sesame seeds for garnish

Instructions:

1. Prepare the cream pancake batter.
2. Whisk in 1-2 tablespoons of matcha green tea powder into the

batter.

3. Cook small pancake rounds until they have a slight green hue.
4. Sandwich sweet red bean paste and a dollop of whipped cream between two pancakes.
5. Sprinkle with sesame seeds for added texture and authenticity.

C. Italian Tiramisu Pancake Stack
Ingredients:

- Cream pancake batter
- Coffee syrup (coffee, sugar)
- Mascarpone cheese
- Cocoa powder
- Dark chocolate shavings

Instructions:

1. Prepare the cream pancake batter.
2. Cook the pancakes until they are golden brown.
3. Drizzle each pancake with a coffee syrup made by dissolving sugar in freshly brewed coffee.
4. Spread a layer of mascarpone cheese between each pancake.
5. Dust the top with cocoa powder and garnish with dark chocolate shavings for a taste reminiscent of classic Tiramisu.

These international delights offer a culinary journey from France to Japan and Italy. Enjoy the diverse and unique flavors inspired by these cultural treasures in the comfort of your own kitchen!

Chapter(11) Brunch Bonanza

A. Creating a Pancake Brunch Spread

Classic Cream Pancakes:

Prepare a batch of the basic cream pancake recipe.

Offer a variety of toppings such as fresh berries, nuts, whipped cream, and maple syrup.

Stuffed Pancakes Bar:

Set up a station with different fillings like chocolate chips, cream cheese, fruit compotes, and nut butters.

Allow guests to customize their pancakes by adding their favorite fillings.

International Flavors Corner:

Feature a selection of international-inspired cream pancakes, such as Tiramisu, Matcha Green Tea, and French Crème Fraîche.

Provide accompanying toppings or sauces that complement each flavor.

Healthier Alternatives Buffet:

Include options like Whole Wheat Pancakes, Oatmeal, and Yogurt Pancakes, and Low-Sugar Pancakes.

Offer a range of fresh fruits, nuts, and yogurt for healthier topping choices.

B. Pairing Cream Pancakes with Savory Brunch Options

Savory Stuffed Pancakes:

Create savory pancake fillings like spinach and feta, smoked salmon and cream cheese, or bacon and cheddar.

Allow guests to enjoy a mix of sweet and savory pancake options.

Pancake Benedicts:

Top cream pancakes with poached eggs, hollandaise sauce, and a sprinkle of fresh herbs for a unique twist on Eggs Benedict.

Pancake Wraps:

Prepare pancake wraps with savory fillings like scrambled eggs, sautéed vegetables, and cheese.

Serve with a side of salsa or avocado for added flavor.

Breakfast Sandwiches:

Use cream pancakes as the "bread" for breakfast sandwiches. Fill with bacon, egg, and cheese for a delicious and portable option.

C. Unique Beverage Pairings

Chai Latte:

Pair cream pancakes with a warm chai latte for a cozy and aromatic brunch experience.

Iced Matcha Tea:

Serve cream pancakes with an iced matcha tea for a refreshing and slightly bitter contrast to the sweetness of the pancakes.

Mimosa Bar:

Create a mimosa bar with different fruit juices and sparkling wine options to complement the diverse flavors of the pancakes.

Coffee Flight:

Offer a selection of coffee options, from bold espresso to creamy lattes, to accompany the various pancake flavors.

A pancake brunch bonanza is the perfect way to celebrate special occasions or enjoy a leisurely weekend morning with friends and family. The combination of sweet and savory options, along with unique beverages, will make your brunch gathering truly memorable.

Chapter(12) Creative Shapes and Sizes

A. Pancake Art: Tips for Shaping and Decorating

Colorful Batter:

Divide the pancake batter into separate bowls and add food coloring to create a palette for your pancake art.

Squeeze Bottles:

Use squeeze bottles to create intricate designs. Fill them with different colored batters and draw shapes, letters, or patterns directly onto the griddle.

Layering Techniques:

Experiment with layering different colored batters to create multi-colored and visually appealing pancakes.

Stencil Fun:

Cut stencils from paper or use cookie cutters as stencils to shape your pancakes into animals, characters, or geometric designs.

Chocolate Drizzle:

Enhance your pancake art by drizzling melted chocolate or colored icing on top for added detail and flavor.

B. Miniature Cream Pancake Stacks for Parties
Ingredients:

- Mini cream pancake batter (scaled-down version of the regular batter)
- Assorted toppings (berries, whipped cream, mini chocolate chips, etc.)
- Toothpicks or mini skewers

Instructions:

1. Prepare a scaled-down version of the cream pancake batter.
2. Cook mini pancakes using a small spoon or squeeze bottle to control the size.
3. Stack mini pancakes on toothpicks or mini skewers, alternating with layers of whipped cream and fresh berries.
4. Garnish the top with a dollop of whipped cream and a sprinkle of mini chocolate chips.
5. Serve as bite-sized pancake stacks at parties or brunch gatherings.

C. Heart-Shaped Pancakes for Special Occasions
Ingredients:

- Cream pancake batter
- Heart-shaped pancake molds or cookie cutters
- Toppings of your choice (fresh fruit, powdered sugar, whipped cream)

Instructions:

1. Prepare the cream pancake batter.
2. Heat a griddle or skillet and lightly grease it.

3. Place heart-shaped pancake molds or cookie cutters on the griddle.
4. Pour the pancake batter into the molds, filling them about halfway.
5. When the edges start to set, carefully remove the molds and flip the pancakes.
6. Cook until the pancakes are golden brown on both sides.
7. Serve with your favorite toppings for a romantic and special breakfast treat.

These creative shapes and sizes add a playful and artistic element to your cream pancakes, making them perfect for entertaining guests or celebrating special occasions. Enjoy the fun of pancake art and share these delightful treats with your loved ones!

Chapter(13) Cooking with Kids

A. Easy Cream Pancake Recipes for Little Chefs
Simple Vanilla Pancakes:

- Ingredients: Cream pancake batter, vanilla extract
- Instructions: Allow kids to mix the batter and add a splash of vanilla extract for extra flavor. Cook on the griddle with adult supervision.

Fruity Delight Pancakes:

- Ingredients: Cream pancake batter, colorful fruit pieces (berries, banana slices)
- Instructions: Kids can place fruit pieces directly onto the cooking pancakes to create fun patterns and designs.

Chocolate Chip Happiness:

- Ingredients: Cream pancake batter, mini chocolate chips
- Instructions: Kids can fold in mini chocolate chips into the batter and help scoop it onto the griddle. Watch as the chocolate melts to create delicious chocolate swirls.

B. Creative Toppings for a Kid-Friendly Twist
Rainbow Sprinkle Fiesta:

- Ingredients: Cream pancake batter, rainbow sprinkles
- Toppings: Whipped cream, more sprinkles
- Instructions: Let kids add rainbow sprinkles directly into the batter. Top the cooked pancakes with whipped cream and extra sprinkles for a colorful delight.

Teddy Bear Pancake Pals:

- Ingredients: Cream pancake batter
- Toppings: Sliced strawberries, banana slices, mini chocolate chips
- Instructions: Shape pancakes into teddy bear faces on the griddle. Kids can use fruit and chocolate chips to create adorable features.

Build-Your-Own Pancake Bar:

- Ingredients: Cream pancake batter, various toppings (chocolate chips, fruit pieces, nuts, whipped cream)
- Instructions: Set up a pancake bar with different toppings, and let kids decorate their own pancakes for a personalized touch.

C. Educational Aspects of Cooking with Children
Math Skills:

- Let kids measure ingredients, count the number of pancakes, or divide toppings evenly for each pancake.

Science Exploration:

- Discuss basic science concepts like mixing ingredients, observing changes during cooking, and understanding heat and temperature.

Fine Motor Skills:

- Whisking, pouring, and flipping pancakes help develop fine motor skills in children.

Reading and Following Directions:

- Have kids read the recipe and follow step-by-step instructions, enhancing their reading and comprehension skills.

Creativity and Imagination:

- Encourage creativity with pancake art, allowing children to express themselves through food.

Cooking with kids not only provides a fun and delicious activity but also offers valuable learning experiences in various subjects. Enjoy the bonding time and delicious results with your little chefs!

Chapter(14) Pancake Hacks and Shortcuts

A. Quick and Easy Cream Pancake Mix
Ingredients:

- 2 cups all-purpose flour
- 1/4 cup sugar
- 1 tablespoon baking powder
- 1/2 teaspoon salt
- 1 cup whipping cream
- 1 cup milk
- 2 large eggs
- 1 teaspoon vanilla extract

Instructions:

1. In a large bowl, whisk together the flour, sugar, baking powder, and salt.
2. In a separate bowl, mix together the whipping cream, milk, eggs, and vanilla extract.
3. Combine the wet and dry ingredients until just mixed.
4. Use this versatile cream pancake mix as a base for various recipes, adding in additional ingredients or toppings as desired.

B. Freezing Pancakes for Later
Cooling Stage:

- Allow cooked pancakes to cool completely on a wire rack to prevent condensation and sogginess.

Single Layer Freezing:

- Place cooled pancakes in a single layer on a baking sheet and freeze until solid.

Stacking for Storage:

- Once frozen, stack the pancakes with sheets of parchment paper between each one to prevent sticking.

Air-Tight Packaging:

- Transfer the stacked pancakes to a freezer bag or airtight container for long-term storage.

Reheating:

- Microwave frozen pancakes for a quick breakfast or warm in the toaster for a crispy texture.

C. Time-Saving Cooking Techniques
One-Bowl Mixing:

- Combine all the dry and wet ingredients in a single bowl for easy preparation and minimal cleanup.

Pre-Measured Dry Mix:

- Pre-measure dry ingredients for several batches and store them in labeled containers for even quicker pancake preparation.

Electric Mixer Assistance:

- Use an electric mixer to quickly blend pancake batter, ensuring a smooth and lump-free consistency.

Sheet Pan Pancakes:

- Pour pancake batter onto a greased sheet pan and bake in the oven for a quicker and hands-free pancake-making experience.

Multi-Tasking:

- While one batch of pancakes cooks, prepare the next batch to optimize your cooking time.

These pancake hacks and shortcuts are designed to streamline the pancake-making process, making it convenient and efficient. Whether you're looking for a quick breakfast or preparing in advance, these tips will help you save time in the kitchen.

Chapter(15) Vegan Cream Pancakes

A. Plant-Based Alternatives for a Creamy Texture
Ingredients:

- 2 cups all-purpose flour
- 2 tablespoons sugar
- 1 tablespoon baking powder
- 1/2 teaspoon salt
- 1 3/4 cups plant-based milk (such as almond, soy, or oat milk)
- 1/4 cup vegetable oil
- 1 teaspoon vanilla extract

Instructions:

1. In a large bowl, whisk together the flour, sugar, baking powder, and salt.
2. Add the plant-based milk, vegetable oil, and vanilla extract to the dry ingredients. Mix until just combined.
3. Cook the pancakes on a greased griddle or skillet until golden brown on both sides.

B. Dairy-Free Whipped Cream Options
Coconut Whipped Cream:
Chill a can of full-fat coconut milk in the refrigerator overnight.
Scoop out the solid coconut cream, leaving behind the liquid.
Whip the coconut cream with a hand mixer until light and fluffy. Sweeten with powdered sugar and vanilla.
Cashew Cream:
Soak cashews in water for a few hours or overnight.
Blend soaked cashews with water, a sweetener of your choice, and vanilla extract until smooth and creamy.
Store-Bought Dairy-Free Whipped Toppings:

Many grocery stores offer ready-made dairy-free whipped cream options made from soy, almond, or coconut.

C. Tips for Veganizing Your Favorite Cream Pancake Recipes

Egg Replacements:

Substitute eggs with ingredients like applesauce, mashed bananas, or commercial egg replacers.

Milk Alternatives:

Replace dairy milk with plant-based alternatives like almond, soy, oat, or coconut milk.

Butter Alternatives:

Use plant-based margarine or coconut oil as a substitute for butter.

Vegan Cream Fillings:

Experiment with vegan cream cheese, coconut cream, or silken tofu blended with sweeteners and flavorings for creamy fillings.

Flaxseed or Chia Egg:

Mix ground flaxseeds or chia seeds with water to create a gel-like consistency, serving as an egg replacement in the batter.

Veganizing cream pancakes is a delicious and inclusive way to enjoy this classic breakfast treat. With the right plant-based ingredients, you can achieve the same creamy texture and delightful flavor in your vegan pancakes.

Chapter(16) Regional Favorites

A. Southern-Style Buttermilk Cream Pancakes
  Ingredients:

- 2 cups all-purpose flour
- 2 tablespoons sugar
- 1 teaspoon baking powder
- 1/2 teaspoon baking soda
- 1/2 teaspoon salt
- 2 cups buttermilk
- 2 large eggs
- 1/4 cup unsalted butter, melted
- 1 teaspoon vanilla extract

Instructions:

1. In a large bowl, whisk together the flour, sugar, baking powder, baking soda, and salt.
2. In a separate bowl, whisk together the buttermilk, eggs, melted butter, and vanilla extract.
3. Add the wet ingredients to the dry ingredients and mix until just combined.
4. Cook on a hot griddle or skillet until golden brown on both sides.

B. Swedish-Inspired Cardamom Cream Pancakes
Ingredients:

- 2 cups all-purpose flour
- 2 tablespoons sugar
- 1 teaspoon baking powder
- 1/2 teaspoon baking soda
- 1/2 teaspoon salt
- 2 cups plant-based milk (such as oat or almond milk)
- 2 tablespoons melted coconut oil
- 1 teaspoon ground cardamom
- 1 teaspoon vanilla extract

Instructions:

- In a bowl, whisk together the flour, sugar, baking powder, baking soda, salt, and ground cardamom.
- Add the plant-based milk, melted coconut oil, and vanilla extract. Mix until just combined.
- Cook on a greased griddle or skillet until the pancakes are golden brown on both sides.

C. Asian Coconut Cream Pancakes
Ingredients:

- 2 cups rice flour
- 2 tablespoons sugar
- 1 teaspoon baking powder
- 1/2 teaspoon salt
- 1 1/2 cups coconut milk
- 1/4 cup water
- 2 tablespoons coconut oil, melted
- Shredded coconut for topping

Instructions:

1. In a bowl, combine the rice flour, sugar, baking powder, and salt.
2. Gradually whisk in the coconut milk, water, and melted coconut oil until the batter is smooth.
3. Cook on a coconut oil-greased griddle until the pancakes are cooked through.
4. Top with shredded coconut for an extra burst of flavor.

These regional favorites bring the distinct flavors of the Southern United States, Sweden, and Asia to your breakfast table. Enjoy the unique tastes and cultural influences with these delicious cream pancake variations!

Chapter(17) Historical Pancake Variations

A. Ancient Grain Cream Pancakes
Ingredients:

- 1 cup spelt flour (or other ancient grain flour)
- 1 tablespoon honey or maple syrup
- 1 teaspoon baking powder
- Pinch of salt
- 1 cup almond milk (or any plant-based milk)
- 1 tablespoon olive oil
- 1 teaspoon vanilla extract

Instructions:

1. In a mixing bowl, combine spelt flour, honey or maple syrup, baking powder, and a pinch of salt.
2. Gradually whisk in almond milk, olive oil, and vanilla extract until the batter is smooth.
3. Cook on a griddle until the pancakes are golden brown on both sides.
4. Serve with honey or fresh berries for a delightful ancient-inspired breakfast.

B. Medieval-Inspired Spiced Cream Pancakes
Ingredients:

- 1 cup barley flour
- 2 tablespoons honey
- 1/2 teaspoon ground cinnamon
- 1/4 teaspoon ground nutmeg
- Pinch of salt

- 1 cup buttermilk
- 1 large egg
- 2 tablespoons melted butter

Instructions:

1. In a bowl, combine barley flour, honey, ground cinnamon, ground nutmeg, and a pinch of salt.
2. Whisk in buttermilk, egg, and melted butter until the batter is well-mixed.
3. Cook on a hot griddle until the pancakes are lightly browned on both sides.
4. Sprinkle with additional cinnamon and serve with a drizzle of honey.

C. Victorian-Era Tea-Infused Cream Pancakes
Ingredients:

- 1 cup whole wheat flour
- 1 tablespoon sugar
- 1 teaspoon baking powder
- Pinch of salt
- 1 cup strong brewed black tea, cooled
- 2 tablespoons melted butter
- 1 large egg
- 1/2 teaspoon vanilla extract

Instructions:

1. In a mixing bowl, combine whole wheat flour, sugar, baking powder, and a pinch of salt.
2. Whisk in strong brewed black tea, melted butter, egg, and vanilla extract until the batter is smooth.
3. Cook on a griddle until the pancakes have a golden-brown

color.

4. Serve with a dollop of clotted cream and a drizzle of honey for a Victorian-inspired treat.

These historical pancake variations take inspiration from ancient, medieval, and Victorian eras, bringing unique flavors and ingredients to your breakfast table. Enjoy a taste of the past with these delightful cream pancake recipes!

Chapter(18) Gluten-Free Extravaganza

A. Almond Flour Cream Pancakes
  Ingredients:

- 1 cup almond flour
- 1 tablespoon coconut flour
- 1 teaspoon baking powder
- Pinch of salt
- 2 tablespoons sugar or sweetener of choice
- 2 large eggs
- 1/2 cup almond milk
- 1 teaspoon vanilla extract

Instructions:

1. In a bowl, combine almond flour, coconut flour, baking powder, salt, and sugar.
2. Whisk in eggs, almond milk, and vanilla extract until a smooth batter forms.
3. Cook on a griddle until the pancakes are golden brown on both sides.
4. Top with your favorite gluten-free toppings, such as berries or dairy-free whipped cream.

B. Coconut Flour and Tapioca Cream Pancakes
Ingredients:

- 1/2 cup coconut flour
- 1/4 cup tapioca flour
- 1 teaspoon baking powder
- Pinch of salt
- 2 tablespoons sugar or sweetener of choice
- 2 large eggs
- 1/2 cup coconut milk
- 2 tablespoons melted coconut oil
- 1 teaspoon vanilla extract

Instructions:

1. In a mixing bowl, combine coconut flour, tapioca flour, baking powder, salt, and sugar.
2. Whisk in eggs, coconut milk, melted coconut oil, and vanilla extract until the batter is well-mixed.
3. Cook on a griddle until the pancakes have a golden-brown color.
4. Serve with tropical fruit toppings or a coconut cream drizzle.

C. Tips for Achieving a Gluten-Free, Yet Fluffy Texture
Blend Flours:
Combine different gluten-free flours to achieve a better texture. Almond flour, coconut flour, and tapioca flour together can provide a nice balance.
Use Leavening Agents:
Include baking powder or baking soda to help the pancakes rise and become fluffy.
Egg Binding:

Eggs play a crucial role in binding gluten-free ingredients. Ensure that your batter has enough eggs for structure.

Liquid Consistency:

Adjust the liquid content in the batter. Gluten-free flours tend to absorb more liquid, so you may need to add more than in a traditional recipe.

Resting Time:

Allow the batter to rest for a few minutes before cooking. This gives the flours time to absorb the liquid and results in a better texture.

Cook at the Right Temperature:

Gluten-free pancakes may take a little longer to cook, so be patient and cook them at a medium heat to ensure they are thoroughly cooked without burning.

Experiment with Add-Ins:

Enhance the flavor and texture by adding ingredients like vanilla extract, cinnamon, or even mashed bananas to the batter.

Enjoy a gluten-free extravaganza with these almond flour and coconut flour cream pancake variations. Follow the tips for achieving a fluffy texture to make your gluten-free pancakes just as delightful as their traditional counterparts!

Chapter(19) Sensational Syrups and Toppings

A. Homemade Flavored Syrups

Vanilla Berry Syrup:

Ingredients: Fresh mixed berries (strawberries, blueberries, raspberries), sugar, water, vanilla extract.

Instructions: Combine berries, sugar, and water in a saucepan. Simmer until the berries break down. Strain, and add vanilla extract.

Cinnamon Maple Syrup:

Ingredients: Maple syrup, ground cinnamon.

Instructions: Warm maple syrup and stir in ground cinnamon. Allow it to infuse for a few minutes before serving.

Citrus Honey Drizzle:

Ingredients: Honey, citrus zest (orange, lemon, or a combination).

Instructions: Mix honey with finely grated citrus zest for a bright and flavorful syrup.

B. Whipped Cream Variations

Coconut Whipped Cream:

Ingredients: Can of coconut cream, powdered sugar, vanilla extract.

Instructions: Chill coconut cream in the refrigerator. Whip until fluffy, adding powdered sugar and vanilla extract.

Maple Bourbon Whipped Cream:

Ingredients: Heavy cream, maple syrup, bourbon.

Instructions: Whip heavy cream until soft peaks form. Gradually add maple syrup and bourbon while continuing to whip.

Chocolate Orange Whipped Cream:

Ingredients: Heavy cream, powdered sugar, cocoa powder, orange zest.

Instructions: Whip heavy cream with powdered sugar. Fold in cocoa powder and finely grated orange zest.

C. Unique Toppings to Elevate Your Cream Pancakes

Pistachio Crunch:

Ingredients: Chopped pistachios, honey.

Instructions: Sprinkle chopped pistachios over whipped cream and drizzle with honey for a delightful crunch.

Lemon Blueberry Compote:

Ingredients: Fresh blueberries, sugar, lemon juice.

Instructions: Cook blueberries with sugar and lemon juice until it forms a compote. Spoon over the pancakes.

Chai Spiced Pecans:

Ingredients: Chopped pecans, chai spice blend (cinnamon, cardamom, ginger, cloves, black pepper), maple syrup.

Instructions: Toast pecans with the chai spice blend. Drizzle with maple syrup.

Rosewater Raspberry Elegance:

Ingredients: Fresh raspberries, rosewater, powdered sugar.

Instructions: Toss raspberries in rosewater and sprinkle with powdered sugar for a fragrant and elegant topping.

Experiment with these sensational syrups, whipped cream variations, and unique toppings to transform your cream pancakes into a gourmet breakfast experience. Combine different flavors for a truly delightful and memorable meal.

Chapter(20) Pancake Photography and Presentation

A. Tips for Instagram-Worthy Pancake Photos

Natural Light:

Shoot your pancakes in natural light to capture the colors and textures effectively.

Close-Up Shots:

Capture the details by taking close-up shots of the texture, toppings, and syrup drizzles.

Varied Angles:

Experiment with different angles to find the most visually appealing perspective.

Backgrounds and Props:

Use aesthetically pleasing backgrounds or props to enhance the overall composition of your photo.

Contrast and Colors:

Create contrast between the pancakes and the background for a visually striking image. Play with vibrant colors.

Action Shots:

Capture a moment in the process, like pouring syrup or cutting into the pancakes.

B. Creative Plating Ideas

Stacked Towers:

Create a tall stack of pancakes and garnish the top for an impressive and appetizing presentation.

Cascading Toppings:

Arrange toppings to cascade down the sides of the pancake stack for a dynamic and visually interesting look.

Mini Pancake Stacks:

Serve mini pancake stacks on individual plates for a cute and elegant presentation.

Pancake Flower Arrangement:

Arrange pancakes in a circular pattern, resembling the petals of a flower. Fill the center with toppings.

Assorted Shapes and Sizes:

Mix different shapes and sizes of pancakes on the plate for a playful and diverse presentation.

C. Food Styling Techniques for Showcasing Cream Pancakes

Drizzle Artfully:

Drizzle syrups or sauces in a deliberate and artful manner, creating visually appealing patterns.

Whipped Cream Peaks:

Pipe whipped cream into decorative peaks for a touch of elegance.

Sprinkle Magic:

Sprinkle toppings evenly and artistically across the pancakes for a balanced and photogenic look.

Color Harmony:

Consider the color harmony of your toppings and background for a visually cohesive presentation.

Garnish with Fresh Herbs or Edible Flowers:

Add a touch of freshness and color with delicate herbs or edible flowers as garnish.

Use Contrasting Plates:

Choose plates that provide a contrast to the color of the pancakes, making them stand out.

Remember, food photography is an art, and creativity is key. Experiment with different styles, angles, and plating techniques to showcase your cream pancakes in the most appealing way possible.

Chapter(21) Interactive Pancake Parties

A. Hosting a Pancake-Making Gathering

Prepare the Pancake Station:

Set up a designated pancake-making station with all the necessary ingredients and equipment. This includes different types of batter, toppings, and cooking stations.

Involve Everyone:

Encourage guests to actively participate in the pancake-making process. Assign roles such as batter mixing, flipping pancakes, or managing toppings.

Variety of Toppings:

Offer a diverse range of toppings, including fruits, nuts, syrups, chocolate chips, and whipped cream. Allow guests to get creative with their combinations.

Personalized Aprons and Utensils:

Provide personalized aprons or utensils for each guest to enhance the festive and communal atmosphere.

Music Playlist:

Create a lively and upbeat playlist to add to the ambiance of the pancake party.

Decorate the Space:

Decorate the space with pancake-themed décor, such as banners, tablecloths, and centerpieces.

B. Pancake Bar Ideas for Customization

Build-Your-Own Pancake Station:

Set up a station with various types of batter (including cream pancake batter), and let guests customize their pancakes with a selection of toppings.

Topping Buffet:

Arrange a topping buffet with bowls of fresh fruits, nuts, sprinkles, syrups, and flavored whipped creams.

Savory and Sweet Options:

Provide both sweet and savory toppings to cater to different preferences. Options could include cheese, bacon, and savory sauces.

Mini Pancake Skewers:

Thread mini pancakes onto skewers along with fruit pieces for a fun and bite-sized pancake experience.

Pancake Ice Cream Sandwich Bar:

Offer a variety of ice cream flavors and toppings for guests to create their own pancake ice cream sandwiches.

C. Tips for Involving Guests in the Cooking Process

Pancake Flipping Contest:

Turn pancake flipping into a friendly competition. Set up a designated area for guests to showcase their flipping skills.

Recipe Cards:

Provide recipe cards with different variations and let guests choose or create their own unique pancake recipes.

Interactive Cooking Demos:

Have a chef or knowledgeable friend conduct short cooking demonstrations, sharing tips and tricks for perfect pancakes.

Pancake Art Station:

Set up a pancake art station with squeeze bottles filled with different colored batters for guests to create artistic designs on their pancakes.

Pancake-Stacking Challenge:

Challenge guests to see who can create the tallest and most stable pancake stack. Offer small prizes for the winners.

Share the Creations:

Set up a designated area for guests to display their finished pancakes. Encourage them to take photos and share their creations on social media.

Interactive pancake parties provide a delightful and engaging experience for guests. By involving everyone in the cooking process and offering a variety of customization options, you'll create lasting memories and delicious pancakes!

Chapter(22) Continuing Your Pancake Journey

A. Resources for Further Exploration

Cookbooks:

Explore cookbooks dedicated to pancake recipes and breakfast delights. Notable titles include "The Joy of Pancakes" and "Pancakes: 72 Sweet and Savory Recipes for the Perfect Stack."

Online Recipe Platforms:

Visit popular recipe websites for a vast array of pancake recipes. Websites like Allrecipes, Food Network, and Bon Appétit often feature creative pancake variations.

YouTube Cooking Channels:

Watch cooking channels on YouTube for step-by-step video tutorials on making different types of pancakes. Channels like Tasty and Food Wishes often feature pancake recipes.

Food Blogs:

Follow food blogs and websites dedicated to breakfast and brunch recipes. Food bloggers often share their own twists on classic pancake recipes.

B. Online Communities for Pancake Enthusiasts

Reddit - r/Pancakes:

Join the Pancakes subreddit to connect with other pancake enthusiasts, share your creations, and gather inspiration from fellow pancake lovers.

Instagram and TikTok:

Explore pancake-related hashtags on Instagram and TikTok to discover a vibrant community of home cooks and professional chefs showcasing their pancake artistry.

Facebook Groups:

Look for Facebook groups focused on pancake making and breakfast lovers. These groups provide a space to exchange recipes, tips, and photos.

C. Challenges and Goals for Your Pancake-Making Skills

30-Day Pancake Challenge:

Challenge yourself to make a different type of pancake every day for a month. Experiment with flavors, shapes, and toppings.

Master a Signature Pancake Recipe:

Work on perfecting a signature pancake recipe that you can proudly call your own. Experiment until you achieve pancake perfection.

International Pancake Tour:

Explore pancakes from around the world. Set a goal to make pancakes inspired by different countries and cultures, expanding your culinary repertoire.

Pancake Art Mastery:

Dive into the world of pancake art. Set a goal to master creating intricate designs and shapes using pancake batter.

Host a Pancake Tasting Event:

Organize a pancake tasting event for friends and family. Challenge yourself to create a diverse and impressive spread of pancakes for everyone to enjoy.

Attend Cooking Classes:

Take pancake-making classes, either in-person or online, to learn new techniques and gain insights from professional chefs.

Continuing your pancake journey involves exploring new recipes, connecting with fellow enthusiasts, and setting personal challenges to enhance your skills. Embrace the joy of pancake making and the endless possibilities it offers!

❖ Conclusion

A. Recap of Key Points

In our exploration of "Whipped Delights: A Guide to Irresistible Cream Pancakes," we covered a range of topics to elevate your pancake-making experience. Here's a quick recap:

Introduction:

Explored the rich history and versatility of pancakes, highlighting the unique qualities that make cream pancakes stand out.

Getting Started:

Discussed essential ingredients and equipment needed for preparing perfect cream pancakes.

Basic Cream Pancake Recipe:

Provided step-by-step instructions, tips for achieving a fluffy texture, and variations for different dietary preferences.

Flavorful Additions:

Explored creative ideas for fresh fruit toppings, crunchy nuts, chocolate swirls, and savory twists to enhance your cream pancakes.

Gourmet Cream Pancake Creations:

Introduced stuffed pancakes, layered pancake cakes, sandwich ideas, and complementary sauces for a gourmet pancake experience.

Special Occasion Cream Pancakes:

Shared festive recipes for holidays and birthdays, adding a touch of celebration to your pancake repertoire.

International Flavors:

Explored exotic flavors, drawing inspiration from Tiramisu, Matcha, and tropical coconut fusions.

Healthier Alternatives:

Provided alternatives like whole wheat, oatmeal, and low-sugar options for guilt-free indulgence.

Troubleshooting Guide:

Addressed common issues and shared tips to perfect your cream pancakes every time.

Conclusion:

Encouraged creativity in pancake making, inspiring you to experiment with various flavors, toppings, and techniques.

B. Encouragement for Creativity in Pancake Making

Embarking on the journey of pancake making is not just about creating a meal; it's about expressing your culinary creativity. Pancakes provide a canvas for flavors, textures, and designs that are as diverse as your imagination. Don't be afraid to think outside the (pancake) box, mix unexpected ingredients, and turn breakfast into a delightful art form.

C. Shareable Final Thoughts and Encouragement to Experiment with Cream Pancakes

"Whipped Delights: A Guide to Irresistible Cream Pancakes" is your passport to a world of pancake possibilities. Cream pancakes offer a luxurious and delightful twist to a classic favorite. As you continue your pancake journey, remember that every flip of the spatula is a chance to explore, innovate, and share joy with those around you.

So go ahead, whip up your favorite cream pancake recipe, adorn it with creative toppings, and share the joy of pancake making with friends and family. Let the aroma of sizzling pancakes and the laughter of shared moments fill your kitchen, creating memories that are as sweet and satisfying as the pancakes themselves. Happy pancake making!

www.ingramcontent.com/pod-product-compliance
Lightning Source LLC
Chambersburg PA
CBHW021801150726
47989CB00004B/1755